TREASURE HUNTER
ACTIVITY BOOK

Chuck Whelon

DOVER PUBLICATIONS, INC.
MINEOLA, NEW YORK

NOTE

Join investigative archaeologist Annabelle Smith, famous explorer Bing Carter, and a host of other treasure hunters and adventurers as they work their way through mazes, labyrinths, and puzzles in order to get the gold—and they'll need your help, so get ready for some treasure hunting! Try to solve all the activities on your own, but if you get stuck, just turn to the Solutions section, which begins on page 39. Don't forget to color the illustrations after you've completed the activities for even more fun.

Copyright

Copyright © 2011 by Dover Publications, Inc.
All rights reserved.

Bibliographical Note

Treasure Hunter Activity Book is a new work, first published by Dover Publications, Inc., in 2011.

International Standard Book Number

ISBN-13: 978-0-486-47878-4
ISBN-10: 0-486-47878-5

Manufactured in the United States by Courier Corporation
47878503
www.doverpublications.com

Annabelle Smith, investigative archaeologist, needs to identify the Roman emperor Adrian on these coins. Adrian is the only one who appears on exactly three coins. Find and circle the three coins which feature Adrian.

1

Twenty valuable, gold coins were lost in this shipwreck. Draw a circle around each of the twenty coins to help the two divers recover them.

Help these treasure hunters through the maze of coins, and past the giant dragon to the exit on the other side.

START

After a lifetime of questing, Sir Beddows finally discovered the location of the Golden Goblet! It's one of a kind—find and circle the only goblet on the table that doesn't have a match.

9

Help these treasure hunters figure out which bandage belongs to the mummy, King Nuthut.

10

There are twelve ancient relics hidden in this picture that this explorer can't wait to get his hands on! Use the guide on the left to help you find and circle them all.

Annabelle Smith needs to crack the code in order to figure out which door is the entrance to the treasure room of the Tomb of Doom. Use the wheel and the symbols above each doorway to help her find the right one.

Wizard Grandhat wants to steal the dragon's treasure, but he must cast a spell to stop each of the three other adventurers first. Find a path to the treasure that passes the other three adventurers.

START

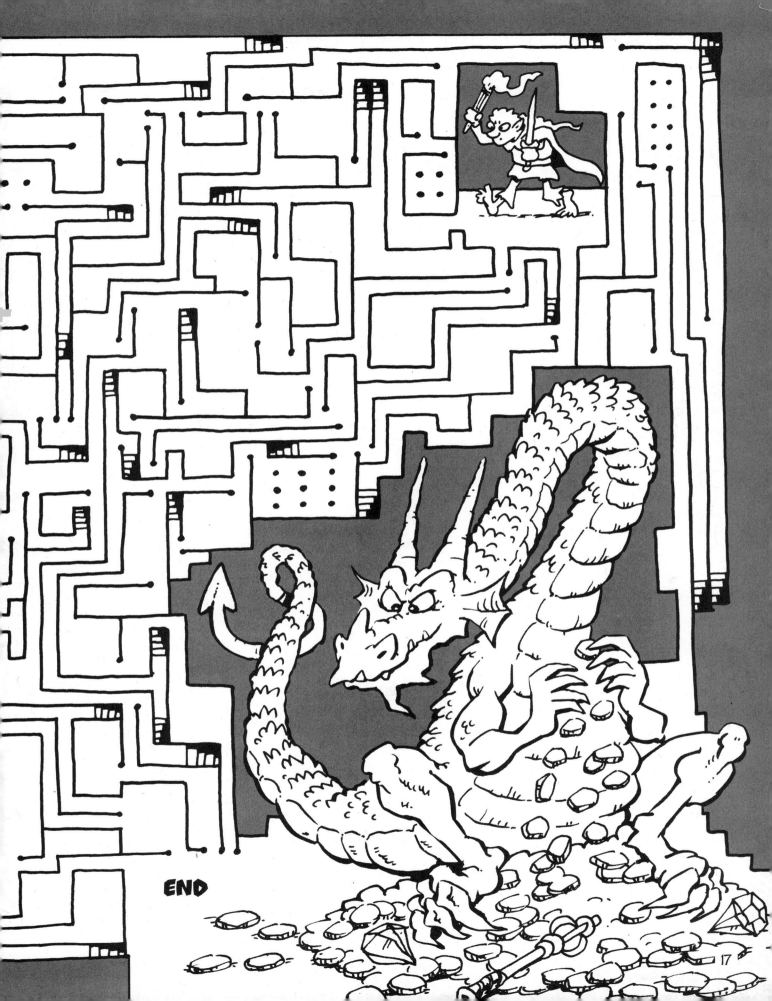

END

17

The goblin king stole all of Gorin Rockfist's gold! Use the maze to help Gorin get to the goblin king.

START

END

19

Use the maze to help Bing Carter get to his truck without running into anyone who might want to steal his treasure!

START

END

One of these skeletons belongs to the Dread Pirate Peterson, and he's sitting on a chest of gold. To find him, follow the clues on the scroll.

He always wore a hat.
He had no beard.
He didn't wear glasses.
He always carried a sword.
He didn't like parrots.
He didn't have a wooden leg
—or an eyepatch.
He did have a hook.
He never used the skull and crossbones symbol.

Solve the maze to help this gold prospector reach his claim.

START

24

END

27

START

29

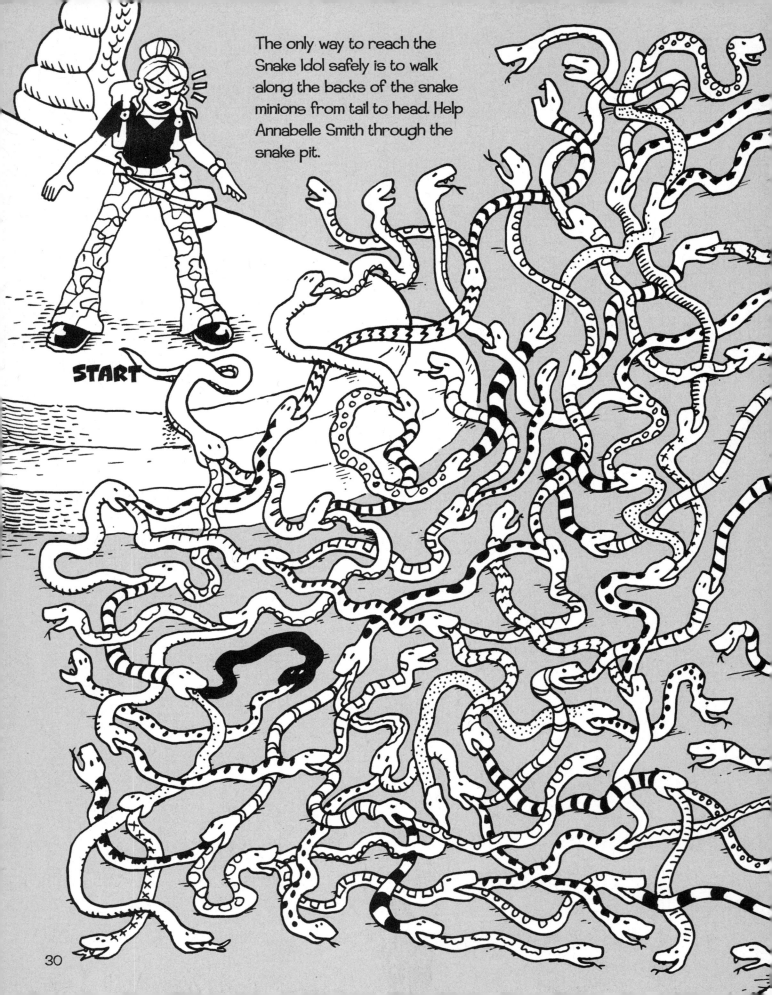

The only way to reach the
Snake Idol safely is to walk
along the backs of the snake
minions from tail to head. Help
Annabelle Smith through the
snake pit.

START

END

31

Help Prince Theseus through the labyrinth. Pick up the 11 golden coins along the way, and rescue Princess Ariadine-but avoid the Minotaur, and don't loose your way by doubling back or crossing your path.

START

32

END

Use the clues to help these pirates figure out which "X" marks the spot.

34

1   2   3   4   5

MILES

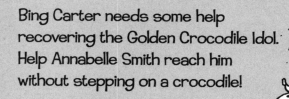

Bing Carter needs some help recovering the Golden Crocodile Idol. Help Annabelle Smith reach him without stepping on a crocodile!

START

END

36

Help Bing Carter cross this floor in the Hidden Temple by following the symbols on his scroll in the correct order, moving only horizontally or vertically.

START

END

Solutions

Page 1

Pages 2-3

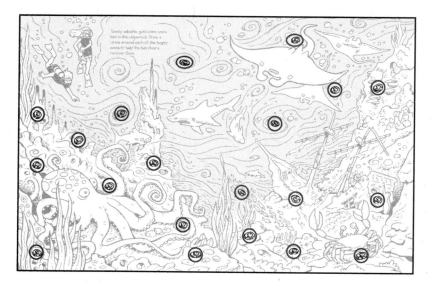

Pages 4-5

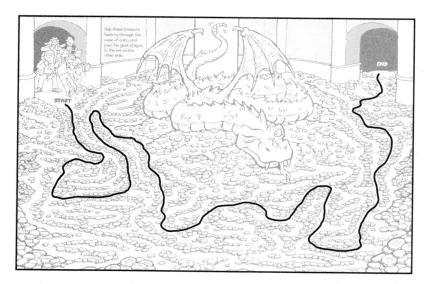

Pages 6-7

Pages 8-9

Pages 10-11

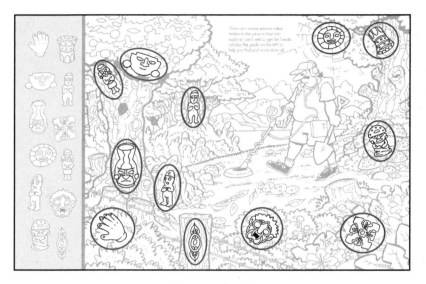

Pages 12-13

Pages 14-15

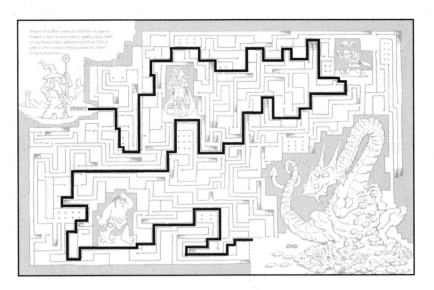

Pages 16-17

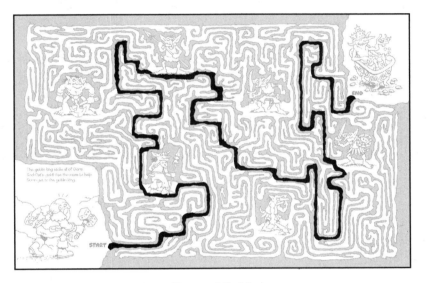

Pages 18-19

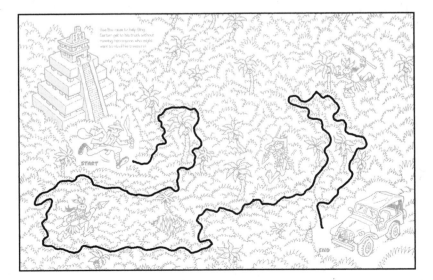

Pages 20-21

Pages 22-23

Pages 24-25

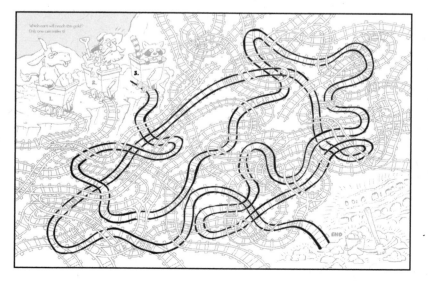

Pages 26-27

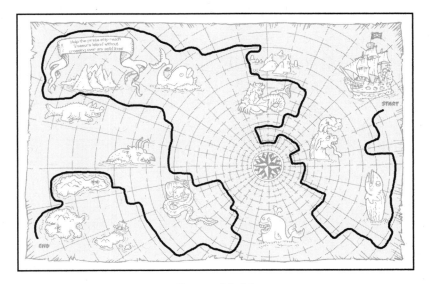

Pages 28-29

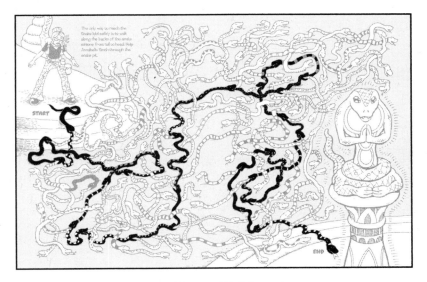

Pages 30-31

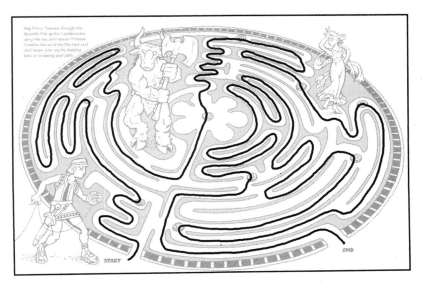

Pages 32-33

Pages 34-35

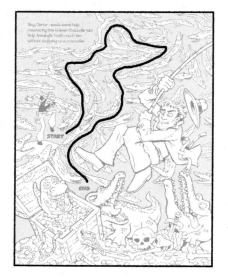

Page 36

Page 37